Air Fryer Cookbook for Beginners

101 Budget Friendly, Quick & Easy 5-Ingredient Air Fryer Recipes, #2020 Edition

© **Sandra Cunningham**

All rights reserved.

ISBN: 9798609784957

Table of Contents

Breakfast & Brunch

- Air Fryer Bagels 4
- Avocado Egg Boats 5
- Bacon-Wrapped Tater Tots 6
- Banana Fritters 7
- Easy Poached Eggs 8
- Easy Sausage Patties 9
- English Breakfast 10
- Grilled Cheese 11
- Hawaiian Pizzas 12
- Mushroom Frittata 13
- Pepperoni Pizza 14
- Pumpkin Steel-Cut Oat 15
- Quick and Easy Doughnuts 16
- Raisin and Apple Dumplings 17
- Sausage Wraps 18
- Scrambled Eggs 19
- Spinach Frittata 20

Poultry

- Bacon-Wrapped Chicken 21
- BBQ Chicken, Gluten-Free 22
- Buffalo Chicken Wings 23
- Cheesy Chicken 24
- Chicken Breast Tenderloins 25
- Chicken Fillet Strips 26
- Chinese Chicken Wings 27
- Chicken Tenders 28
- Crispy Chicken Sliders 29
- Garlic Herb Turkey Breast 30

Honey-Lime Chicken Wings ... 31
Whole Chicken ... 32
Tarragon Chicken ... 33

Beef

Beef and Potato ... 34
Beef Roll-Ups ... 35
Breaded Beef Schnitzel ... 36
Cheeseburger 'Mini' Sliders ... 37
Quick and Easy Rib Eye Steak ... 38
Roast Beef ... 49
Montreal Steak ... 40

Pork & Lamb

Bacon-Wrapped Pork Tenderloin ... 41
Bratwurst and Veggies ... 42
Crispy Dumplings ... 43
Pork Taquitos ... 44
Ranch-Style Pork Chops ... 45
Southern Fried Pork Chops ... 46
Stuffed Pork Chops ... 47
Lamb Ribs Saltimbocca ... 48

Seafood

Breaded Coconut Shrimp ... 49
Breaded Cod Sticks ... 50
Cajun Salmon ... 51
Cajun Shrimp ... 52
Cod Fish Nuggets ... 53
Creamy Salmon ... 54
Crumbled Fish ... 55
Easy Crab Sticks ... 56
Fish Surprise ... 57

Snacks

Avocado and Bacon Fries ... 58
Bacon-Wrapped Hot Dogs ... 59

Cheesy Hot Dogs 60
Jalapeno Poppers 61
Mozzarella Cheese Sticks 62
Pigs in a Blanket 63
Potato Skin Wedges 64
Potato Fat-Free Fries 65

Desserts

Air-Fried Plantains 66
Air-Fried Smores 67
Apple Chips 68
Banana Smores 69
Cherry Pie 70
Easy Bacon 71
Marshmallow Turnovers 72
Funnel Cake Bites 73
Healthy Pop-Tarts 74
Molten Lava Cakes 75
Plain Cheesecake 76
Yogurt Pineapple Sticks 77

Air Fryer Bagels

Servings: 4

Ingredients:
- Plain Greek yogurt - zero-fat (1 cup)
- Self-rising flour (1 cup)
- Egg (1 for the egg wash)
- Desired Garnishes: Sesame or poppy seeds

Steps Used to Prepare:
1. Set the Air Fryer at 330° Fahrenheit ahead of baking time.
2. Whisk the yogurt and flour to form a tacky dough.
3. Dust a preparation surface and roll the dough into a ball, slicing it into four sections.
4. Roll each one into bagel shapes and pinch to close. Prepare two at a time, brushing the tops with egg wash.
5. Set the timer for ten minutes after arranging the bagels in the cooker.
6. For the toppings, brush with a portion of melted butter and season as desired.

Avocado Egg Boats

Servings: 2

Ingredients:
- Avocado (1)
- Large eggs (2)
- *Optional Garnishes*:
- Freshly chopped chives
- Parsley
- Pepper

Steps Used to Prepare:
1. Set the Air Fryer temperature setting at 350º Fahrenheit.
2. Discard the pit from the avocado. Slice and scoop out part of the flesh and add the seasonings.
3. Break an egg into each half and place it in the Air Fryer. Set the timer for six minutes.
4. Serve using toppings of your choice.

Bacon-Wrapped Tater Tots

Servings: 4

Ingredients:
- Sour cream (3 tbsp.)
- Medium-sliced bacon (1 lb.)
- Bag of crispy tater tots (1 large)
- Scallions (4)
- Shredded cheddar cheese (.5 cup)

Steps Used to Prepare:
1. Set the Air Fryer at 400º Fahrenheit.
2. Wrap each of the tots in bacon and place them into the fryer basket. Keep them in a single layer.
3. Set the timer for eight minutes.
4. Arrange the tots on a plate. Serve with the scallions and cheese garnish. Add a dash of sour cream.

Banana Fritters

Servings: 8

Ingredients:
- Vegetable oil (3 tbsp.)
- Breadcrumbs (.75 cup)
- Corn flour (3 tbsp.)
- Ripe peeled bananas (8)
- Egg white (1)

Steps Used to Prepare:
1. Warm the Air Fryer to reach 356° Fahrenheit.
2. Use the low-heat temperature setting to warm a skillet. Pour in the oil and toss in the breadcrumbs. Cook until golden brown.
3. Coat the bananas with the flour. Dip them into the whisked egg white and cover with the breadcrumbs.
4. Arrange the prepared bananas in a single layer of the basket and place the fritter cakes onto a bunch of paper towels to drain before serving.

Easy Poached Eggs

Servings: 1

Ingredients:
- Boiling water (3 cups)
- Large egg (1)

Steps Used to Prepare:
1. Set the Air Fryer at 390º Fahrenheit.
2. Pour boiling water into the Air Fryer basket.
3. Break the egg into a dish and slide it into the water. Set the basket into the fryer.
4. Set the timer for 3 minutes. When ready, scoop the poached egg into a plate using a slotted spoon.
5. Serve with a serving of toast to your liking.

Easy Sausage Patties

Servings: 4

Ingredients:
- Sausage patties (12 oz pkg.)

Steps Used to Prepare:
1. Warm the Air Fryer at 400º Fahrenheit.
2. Arrange the patties in a single layer, working in batches if needed.
3. Set the timer for five minutes.
4. Flip the sausage over and cook until they reach 160º Fahrenheit on an instant-read thermometer or about three minutes.

English Breakfast

Servings: 4

Ingredients:
- Sausages (8)
- Eggs (4)
- Bacon slices (8)
- Baked beans (16 oz. can)
- Toast (8 slices)

Steps Used to Prepare:
1. Arrange the bacon and sausage in the Air Fryer basket. Set the timer for ten minutes at 320º Fahrenheit.
2. Add the beans into a ramekin/heat-safe dish. In a second dish, add the whisked eggs.
3. Increase the setting to 390º Fahrenheit.
4. Place them in the basket and set the timer for another ten minutes.
5. Stir and serve when ready.

Grilled Cheese Sandwiches

Servings: 2

Ingredients:
- Sharp cheddar cheese (.5 cup)
- White bread or brioche (4 slices)
- Melted butter (.25 cup)

Steps Used to Prepare:
1. Set the Air Fryer at 360º Fahrenheit.
2. Butter all slices of bread (both sides). Assemble each sandwich and arrange them in the fryer basket.
3. Prepare for 5-7 minutes and serve immediately for the best taste results.

Hawaiian Pizzas

Servings: 12

Ingredients:
- Thomas' Light Multi-Grain English Muffins (1 pkg.)
- Pizza sauce (1 cup)
- Canadian Bacon (.5 cup)
- Crushed pineapple (.25 cup)
- Shredded mozzarella cheese (1-2 cups)

Steps Used to Prepare:
1. Set the fryer at 355º Fahrenheit.
2. Gently, using your finger, separate the English muffins.
3. Place a sheet of foil inside the Air Fryer, making sure that air is still able to circulate. Spritz it with a non-stick cooking spray.
4. Add the halves of the English muffins to the fryer (as many as can fit neatly).
5. Top each half with sauce, Canadian bacon, and pineapple, and shredded cheese.
6. Air-fry for 5 minutes. It's essential to check them after about 3 minutes to be sure all toppings are still cooking evenly.
7. Remove and serve.

Mushroom Onion Cheese Frittata

Servings: 2

Ingredients:
- Olive oil (1 tbsp.)
- Mushrooms (2 cups)
- Onion (1 small)
- Eggs (3)
- Grated cheese (50 g or .5 cup)
- *Also Needed*: 1 Skillet

Steps Used to Prepare:
1. Warm the Air Fryer at 320° Fahrenheit.
2. Prepare a skillet (medium heat) and pour in the oil.
3. Chop the mushrooms and onions. Toss into the pan and sauté for about five minutes before adding them to the Air Fryer.
4. Whisk the eggs and salt. Dump it into the fryer with a sprinkle of cheese.
5. Set the timer for 10 minutes and remove to serve.

Pepperoni, Egg, and Cheese Pizza

Servings: 1

Ingredients:
- Oregano (.5 tsp.)
- Basil (.5 tsp.)
- Eggs (2)
- Shredded mozzarella cheese (2 tbsp.)
- Thinly sliced pepperoni (4 pieces)
- Also Needed: 1 ramekin

Steps Used to Prepare:
1. Whisk the eggs, basil, and oregano.
2. Pour the eggs into the ramekin, and add the pepperoni and cheese.
3. Arrange the ramekin in the Air Fryer for three minutes and serve.

Pumpkin Steel-Cut Oat

Servings: 4

Ingredients:
- Water (1.5 cups)
- Pumpkin puree (.5 cup)
- Stevia (3 tbsp.)
- Pumpkin pie spice (1 tsp.)
- Steel-cut oats (.5 cup)

Steps Used to Prepare:
1. Heat the Air Fryer at 360º Fahrenheit to preheat.
2. Toss in and mix the fixings into the Air Fryer.
3. Set the timer for 20 minutes.
4. When it's ready, portion the oatmeal into bowls and serve.

Quick and Easy Doughnuts

Servings: 4

Ingredients:
- Flaky jumbo refrigerated dough biscuits (1 can)
- Ground cinnamon (1.5 tsp.)
- White granulated sugar (.5 cup)
- Coconut oil or ghee (as needed)

Steps Used to Prepare:
1. Set the Air Fryer at 350º Fahrenheit.
2. Arrange the biscuits on a cutting board. Use a one-inch biscuit cutter to remove the centers.
3. Grease the basket with the oil/ghee.
4. Whisk the sugar and cinnamon.
5. Air-fry the doughnuts for five to six minutes. Fry the holes for three to four minutes.
6. Transfer to a dish and brush using the butter, garnishing using a sprinkle of the cinnamon/sugar mixture.

Raisin and Apple Dumplings

Servings: 2

Ingredients:
- Raisins (2 tbsp.)
- Small apples (2)
- Brown sugar (1 tbsp.)
- Puff pastry (2 sheets)
- Melted butter (2 tbsp.)

Steps Used to Prepare:
1. Warm the Air Fryer to reach 356° Fahrenheit.
2. Peel and core the apples. Combine the raisins and sugar. Place the apples on the pastry sheets and fill with the raisin mixture.
3. Fold the pastry over to cover the fixings. Place them on a piece of foil so they won't fall through the fryer. Brush them with melted butter.
4. Air-fry until they're golden brown (25 minutes).
5. *Note*: It's best to prepare using tiny apples.

Sausage Wraps

Servings: 8

Ingredients:
- Crescent roll dough (8-count can)
- American cheese (2 slices)
- Heat and Serve Sausages (8)
- Wooden skewers (8)
- Optional for Dipping: BBQ sauce/ketchup/syrup

Steps Used to Prepare:
1. Set the Air Fryer to 380º Fahrenheit.
2. Open the sausages, and separate the rolls.
3. Slice the cheese into quarters, and add the pieces starting on the widest part of the triangle to the tip. Add the sausage.
4. Gather each end and roll-over the sausage and cheese. Pinch each side together. Add these in two batches to the fryer.
5. Cook for 3-4 minutes.
6. Remove from the fryer and add a skewer. Set it out for serving with the desired garnish.

Scrambled Eggs

Servings: 1

Ingredients:
- Butter (for the fryer basket)
- Eggs (2)
- Black pepper (as desired)
- Optional: Cheese and tomatoes

Steps Used to Prepare:
1. Warm the Air Fryer at 285º Fahrenheit for about five minutes.
2. Melt a small portion of butter, spreading it out evenly.
3. Whisk and dump the eggs and any other desired fixings desired.
4. Open the fryer every few minutes to whisk the eggs.
5. Serve with a serving of toast or have a scrambled egg sandwich.

Spinach Frittata

Servings: 1-2

Ingredients:
- Spinach (⅓ of 1 pkg.)
- Red onion (1 small)
- Mozzarella cheese
- Eggs (3)

Steps Used to Prepare:
1. Heat the Air Fryer at 356º Fahrenheit for at least three minutes.
2. Pour the oil into a baking pan for one minute.
3. Mince and toss in the onions. Sauté for two to three minutes. Toss in the spinach and sauté another three to five minutes.
4. Whip in the eggs, add the seasonings, cheese, and add to the pan.
5. Air Fry for 8 minutes. Flavor with salt and pepper if you wish.

Bacon-Wrapped Chicken

Servings: 3

Ingredients:
- Breast of chicken (1)
- Unsmoked bacon (6 strips)
- Soft garlic cheese (1 tbsp.)

Steps Used to Prepare:
1. Slice the chicken into six portions.
2. Spread the garlic cheese over each bacon strip. Add a piece of chicken to each one. Roll and secure with a toothpick.
3. Prepare the Air Fryer ahead of fry time for about three minutes.
4. Arrange the wraps in the fryer basket. Air-fry them for about 15 minutes.

BBQ Chicken, Gluten-Free

Servings: 4

Ingredients:
- Boneless - skinless chicken breast (2 large)
- Seasoned flour/Gluten-free seasoned flour (.5 cup)
- Barbecue sauce (1 cup)
- Olive oil cooking spray

Steps Used to Prepare:
1. Heat the Air Fryer to reach 390º Fahrenheit.
2. Chop the chicken into bite-size chunks and place it in a mixing bowl. Coat the chunks with the seasoned flour.
3. Lightly spritz the basket of the Air Fryer with olive oil cooking spray and evenly pour the chicken into the cooker.
4. Set the timer for 8 minutes.
5. Open the Air Fryer, coat the basket with olive oil spray, and flip the chicken as needed.
6. Air-fry the chicken for eight more minutes. Be sure its internal reading is at least 165º Fahrenheit.
7. Place the chicken into a dish and add the sauce.
8. Line the Air Fryer with a sheet of foil or add the chicken back to the fryer and cook for another 3 minutes until the sauce is warmed and the chicken is a bit crispier and more coated. Serve.

Buffalo Chicken Wings

Servings: 2-3

Ingredients:
- Butter - melted (1 tbsp.)
- Chicken wings (5 /14 oz.)
- Cayenne pepper (2 tsp. or to taste)
- Red hot sauce (2 tbsp.)
- *Optional*: Garlic powder (.5 tsp.)

Steps Used to Prepare:
1. Heat the Air Fryer temperature to reach 356º Fahrenheit.
2. Slice the wings into three sections (end tip, middle joint, and drumstick). Pat each one thoroughly dry using a paper towel.
3. Combine the pepper, salt, garlic powder, and cayenne pepper on a platter. Lightly cover the wings with the powder.
4. Arrange the chicken onto the wire rack and bake for 15 minutes, turning once at 7 minutes.
5. Combine the hot sauce with the melted butter in a dish to garnish the baked chicken when it is time to be served.

Cheesy Chicken

Servings: 4

Ingredients:
- Chicken breasts (4 thin/2 breasts pounded)
- Milk (1 cup)
- Panko breadcrumbs (.5 cup.
- Shaved Parmesan-Asiago cheese blend (.75 to 1 cup)
- Pepper (as desired)

Steps Used to Prepare:
1. Set the Air Fryer temperature at 400º Fahrenheit. Lightly spritz the basket with a non-stick cooking oil spray.
2. Add the milk, chicken, and pepper into a bowl to marinate for about ten minutes.
3. Prepare a shallow dish with the breadcrumbs and cheese.
4. Dredge the chicken through the mixture and place it in the basket of the fryer.
5. Cook it in batches, lightly spraying the tops with the oil spray.
6. Set the timer for eight minutes, and flip the breasts about halfway through the cycle at four minutes.
7. Reheat the first batch for about one minute if desired and serve.

Chicken Breast Tenderloins

Servings: 4

Ingredients:
- Butter/vegetable oil (2 tbsp.)
- Breadcrumbs (3.33 tbsp.)
- Egg (1)
- Chicken tenderloins (8)

Steps Used to Prepare:
1. Heat the Air Fryer temperature to 356º Fahrenheit.
2. Combine the breadcrumbs and oil - stirring until the mixture crumbles.
3. Whisk the egg and dredge the chicken through the egg, shaking off the excess.
4. Dip each piece of chicken into the crumbs and evenly coat.
5. Set the timer for 12 minutes.

Chicken Fillet Strips

Servings: 4

Ingredients:
- Chicken fillets (1 lb.)
- Paprika (1 tsp.)
- Heavy cream (1 tbsp.)
- Black pepper (.5 tsp.)
- Butter (as needed)

Steps Used to Prepare:
1. Heat the Air Fryer at 365º Fahrenheit.
2. Slice the fillets into strips and dust with salt and pepper.
3. Add a light coating of butter to the basket.
4. Arrange the strips in the basket and air-fry for six minutes.
5. Flip the strips and continue frying for another five minutes.
6. When done, garnish with the cream and paprika. Serve warm.

Chinese Chicken Wings

Servings: 2

Ingredients:
- Chicken wings (4)
- Chinese spice (1 tbsp.)
- Mixed spices - your choice (1 tbsp.)
- Soy sauce (1 tbsp.)

Steps Used to Prepare:
1. Warm the Air Fryer to 356º Fahrenheit.
2. Add the seasonings into a large mixing bowl, stirring thoroughly. Pour it over the chicken wings until each piece is covered.
3. Put some aluminum foil on the base of the fryer, and add the chicken sprinkling any remnants over the chicken. Air-fry it for 15 minutes.
4. Flip the chicken and air-fry for another 15 minutes at 392º Fahrenheit.

Coconut-Crusted Chicken Tenders

Servings: 4

Ingredients:
- Eggs (3)
- Chicken tenders (1 lb.)
- Cornstarch (1 cup)
- Sweetened shredded coconut (2 cups)
- Cayenne pepper (1 tsp.)

Steps Used to Prepare:
1. Set the Air Fryer temperature at 360º Fahrenheit.
2. Prepare three dishes. In the first one, add the cornstarch and cayenne with any other desired seasonings. In the second bowl, add the eggs. Lastly, add the coconut in the third dish.
3. Dredge the chicken through the cornstarch, egg, and coconut.
4. Lightly spritz the fryer basket with a cooking oil spray as needed.
5. Set the timer for 8 minutes and air-fry until it's golden brown before serving.

Crispy Chicken Sliders

Servings: 6 = 12 sliders

Ingredients:
- Tyson Crispy Chicken Strips (1 pkg.)
- Sweet Hawaiian Rolls (1 pkg.)
- *Optional Ingredients*:
- Spinach leaves
- Tomatoes
- Honey mustard

Steps Used to Prepare:
1. Place the six chicken strips in the Air Fryer basket with a coating of olive oil spray. Cook at 390º Fahrenheit for 8 minutes.
2. Slice the rolls in half and top them with honey mustard, spinach, and tomatoes or other toppings of your choice.
3. Slice the chicken strips into chunks and place them on the rolls.

Garlic Herb Turkey Breast

Servings: 6

Ingredients:
- Turkey breast (2 lb.)
- Melted butter (4 tbsp.)
- Garlic (3 cloves)
- Thyme (1 tsp.)
- Rosemary (1 tsp.)

Steps Used to Prepare:
1. Warm the Air Fryer to reach 375° Fahrenheit.
2. Pat the turkey breast dry. Mince the garlic and chop the rosemary and thyme.
3. Melt the butter and mix with the garlic, thyme, and rosemary in a small mixing bowl. Brush the butter over turkey breast.
4. Place in the Air Fryer basket, skin side up, and cook for 40 minutes or until internal temperature reaches 160° Fahrenheit, flipping halfway through.
5. Wait for five minutes before slicing.

Honey-Lime Chicken Wings

Servings: 4

Ingredients:
- Chicken wings (2 lb.)
- Lime juice (2 tbsp.)
- Honey (.25 cup)
- Lime zest (1 tbsp.)
- Garlic clove (1 pressed)

Steps Used to Prepare:
1. Warm the Air Fryer at 360° Fahrenheit.
2. Whisk the garlic, honey, and lime juice and zest. Toss in the wings and cover with the mixture.
3. Prepare the wings in batches. Cook for 25-30 minutes until they're crispy. Shake the basket at 8-minute intervals.
4. Serve and garnish as desired.

Rotisserie-Style, Whole Chicken

Servings: 4

Ingredients:
- Olive oil (2 tsp. or as needed)
- Whole chicken (6-7 lb.)
- Seasoned salt (1 tbsp.)

Steps Used to Prepare:
1. Set the Air Fryer at 350º Fahrenheit.
2. Coat the chicken with oil and a sprinkle of salt.
3. Arrange the chicken in the Air Fryer – skin-side down.
4. Cook for 30 minutes. Flip the chicken over and air-fry for another 30 minutes.
5. Wait for ten minutes before slicing
6. *Note*: This recipe is for chickens under 6 lb. for a 3.7-quart Air Fryer.

Tarragon Chicken

Servings: 1

Ingredients:
- Skinless/boneless chicken breast (1)
- Freshly cracked ground black pepper (.125 tsp.)
- Unsalted butter (.5 tsp.)
- Kosher salt (.125 tsp.)
- Dried tarragon (.25 cup)
- Also Needed: Aluminum foil (12x14-inch piece)

Steps Used to Prepare:
1. Warm the oven in advance to reach 390º Fahrenheit.
2. Arrange the chicken in the foil with the tarragon, butter, salt, and pepper.
3. Loosely wrap the foil for minimal airflow.
4. Air-fry the chicken packs for 12 minutes in the basket.

Beef and Potato

Servings: 4

Ingredients:
- Mashed potatoes (3 cups)
- Ground beef (1 lb.)
- Eggs (2)
- Garlic powder (2 tbsp.)
- Sour cream (1 cup)

Steps Used to Prepare:
1. Set the Air Fryer to reach 390º Fahrenheit.
2. Combine all of the fixings in a mixing container. Scoop it into a heat-safe dish.
3. Arrange in the fryer to cook for two minutes.
4. Serve for lunch or a quick dinner.

Beef Roll-Ups

Servings: 4

Ingredients:
- Provolone cheese (6 slices)
- Beef flank steak (2 lbs.)
- Pesto (3 tbsp.)
- Baby spinach (.75 cup)
- Roasted red bell peppers (3 oz.)

Steps Used to Prepare:
1. Heat the Air Fryer at 400º Fahrenheit.
2. Slice the steak. Add the pesto and butter evenly on the meat.
3. Layer in the spinach, peppers, and cheese about ¾ of the way down through the roll-up. Roll the mixture. Secure it with skewers or toothpicks.
4. Air-fry for 14 minutes. Turn the beef halfway through the cooking process.
5. Wait for at least ten minutes before slicing to serve.

Breaded Beef Schnitzel

Servings: 1

Ingredients:
- Olive oil (2 tbsp.)
- Thin beef schnitzel (1)
- Gluten-free breadcrumbs (.5 cup)
- Egg (1)

Steps Used to Prepare:
1. Heat the Air Fryer a couple of minutes (356º Fahrenheit).
2. Combine the breadcrumbs and oil in a shallow bowl. Whisk the egg in another mixing container.
3. Dip the beef into the egg, and then the breadcrumbs. Arrange in the basket of the Air Fryer.
4. Air-fry 12 minutes and serve.

Cheeseburger 'Mini' Sliders

Servings: 3

Ingredients:
- Cheddar cheese (6 slices)
- Ground beef (1 lb.)
- Freshly cracked black pepper and salt (as desired)
- Dinner rolls (6)

Steps Used to Prepare:
1. Warm the Air Fryer ahead of fry time to 390º Fahrenheit.
2. Shape six (2.5-oz.) patties and dust with the pepper and salt
3. Arrange the burgers in the fryer basket and cook for ten minutes.
4. Take them out of the cooker and add the cheese.
5. Return them to the basket for another minute until the cheese melts.

Quick and Easy Rib Eye Steak

Servings: 1

Ingredients:
- Unchilled steak (1 @ about 2 lb.)
- Olive oil (1 tbsp.)
- Steak Rub: Salt and pepper mix (1 tbsp. As desired)
- Baking pan also needed to fit into the basket

Steps Used to Prepare:
1. Press the "M" button for the French Fries icon. Adjust the time to four minutes at 400º Fahrenheit.
2. Rub the steak with the oil and seasonings. Arrange the steak in the basket and air-fry for 14 minutes. (Flip it over after seven minutes.)
3. Place the rib eye on a platter, and let it rest for ten minutes.
4. Slice it and garnish the way you like it.

Roast Beef

Servings: 6

Ingredients:
- Garlic powder (.5 tsp.)
- Oregano (.5 tsp.)
- Dried thyme (1 tsp.)
- Olive oil (1 tbsp.)
- Round roast (2 lb.)

Steps Used to Prepare:
1. Heat the Air Fryer at 330º Fahrenheit.
2. Combine the spices. Brush the oil over the beef, and rub it using the spice mixture.
3. Add to a baking dish and arrange it in the Air Fryer basket for 30 minutes. Turn it over and continue cooking 25 more minutes.
4. Wait for a few minutes before slicing.
5. Serve on your choice of bread or plain with a delicious side dish.

Sweet and Spicy Montreal Steak

Servings: 2

Ingredients:
- Sirloin steaks (2 boneless)
- Brown sugar (1 tbsp.)
- Montreal steak seasoning (1 tbsp.)
- Crushed red pepper (1 tsp.)
- Olive oil (1 tbsp.)

Steps Used to Prepare:
1. Set the temperature of the Air Fryer at 390º Fahrenheit.
2. Prepare the steaks with oil. Rub them with the desired seasonings.
3. Arrange the steaks in the basket and set the timer for three minutes.
4. Flip the steak over and air-fry for another three minutes.
5. Cool and slice it into strips before serving.

Bacon-Wrapped Pork Tenderloin

Servings: 4-6

Ingredients:
- Pork tenderloin (1 lb.)
- Dijon mustard (1-2 tbsp.)
- Bacon (3-4 strips)

Steps Used to Prepare:
1. Set the Air Fryer temperature at 360º Fahrenheit.
2. Coat the tenderloin with the mustard and wrap with the bacon.
3. Air-fry them for 15 minutes. Flip and cook 10 to 15 more minutes.
4. Serve with your favorite sides.

Bratwurst and Veggies

Servings: 6

Ingredients:
- Bratwurst (Approx. 5 links/1 pkg.)
- Red and green bell pepper (1 each)
- Onion - red or purple (.25 cup)
- Gluten-free Cajun seasoning (.5 tbsp.)

Steps Used to Prepare:
1. Warm the unit to reach 390° Fahrenheit.
2. Line the Air Fryer with foil, if preferred.
3. Slice and add in the vegetables.
4. Slice the bratwurst into about 0.5-inch size rounds, and place on top of the veggies.
5. Evenly sprinkle the seasoning on top.
6. Air-fry for 10 minutes. Carefully open and stir or mix.
7. Air-fry for another 10 minutes before serving.

Crispy Dumplings

Servings: 2

Ingredients:
- Ground pork (.5 lb.)
- Olive oil (1 tbsp.)
- Black pepper and salt (.5 tsp. each)
- Dumpling wrappers (half of 1 pkg.)

Steps Used to Prepare:
1. Set the Air Fryer temperature setting at 390º Fahrenheit.
2. Mix the fixings together.
3. Prepare each dumpling using two teaspoons of the pork mixture.
4. Seal the edges with a portion of water to make the triangle form.
5. Lightly spritz the Air Fryer basket using a cooking oil spray as needed. Add the dumplings to air-fry for eight minutes.
6. Serve when they're ready.

Pork Taquitos

Servings: 10

Ingredients:
- Cooked shredded pork tenderloin or chicken (3 cups)
- Fat-free shredded mozzarella (2.5 cups)
- Flour tortillas (10 small)
- Lime juice (1 lime)

Steps Used to Prepare:
1. Set the Air Fryer at 380º Fahrenheit.
2. Sprinkle the juice over the pork.
3. Microwave five of the tortillas at a time (putting a damp paper towel over them for 10 seconds). Add three ounces of pork and ¼ of a cup of cheese to each tortilla.
4. Tightly roll the tortillas. Line the tortillas onto a greased foil-lined pan.
5. Spray an even coat of cooking oil spray over the tortillas.
6. Air Fry for 7 to 10 minutes or until the tortillas are a golden color, flipping halfway through.

Ranch-Style Pork Chops

Servings: 4

Ingredients:
- Center-cut - 1-inch boneless pork chops (4)
- Dry ranch salad dressing mix - ex. Hidden Valley (2 tsp.)
- Also Needed: Aluminum foil and cooking oil spray

Steps Used to Prepare:
1. Warm the Air Fryer to 390º Fahrenheit.
2. Lightly spray both sides of the chops and the inside of the Air Fryer basket using a cooking oil spray. Sprinkle both sides with the ranch seasoning mix and let it rest at room temperature for ten minutes.
3. Place the chops in the Air Fryer, working in batches if necessary, to ensure the fryer isn't overcrowded.
4. Cook for five minutes. Flip the chops and cook five minutes more. Let it rest on a foil-covered plate for an additional five minutes before serving.

Southern Fried Pork Chops

Servings: 5

Ingredients:
- Pork chops (4)
- Buttermilk (3 tbsp.)
- All-purpose flour (.25 cup)
- Seasoning salt
- Freshly cracked black pepper (as desired)

Steps Used to Prepare:
1. Set the fryer at 380º Fahrenheit.
2. Rinse and dry the chops using a paper towel. Season using the pepper and seasoning salt.
3. Drizzle the chops with the buttermilk and toss into a zipper-type bag with the flour. Marinate for 30 minutes.
4. Arrange the chops in the fryer (stacking is okay). Spritz using a cooking oil spray.
5. Air-fry the chops for 15 minutes (380º Fahrenheit). Flip after the first 10 minutes.
6. Serve with your favorite side dishes.

Stuffed Pork Chops

Servings: 3

Ingredients:
- Thick-cut pork chops (3)
- Mushrooms (7)
- Lemon juice (1 tbsp.)
- Almond flour (1 tbsp.)

Steps Used to Prepare:
1. Heat the Air Fryer to reach 350º Fahrenheit.
2. Arrange the pork chops in the Air Fryer. Set the timer for 15 minutes.
3. Chop and sauté the mushrooms for three minutes and spritz with lemon juice.
4. Toss in the flour and herbs. Continue to sauté for four minutes and set aside.
5. Prepare five sheets of foil for the chops. Arrange the chops on the foil and add some of the mushroom fixings.
6. Carefully fold the foil to seal in the chop and juices.
7. Add the chops in the Air Fryer for 30 minutes.

Lamb Ribs - Saltimbocca

Servings: 4

Ingredients:
- Mozzarella cheese (2 balls)
- Lamb racks (2 lb.)
- Thinly sliced pieces of prosciutto (4)
- Sage leaves (4)
- Olive oil (2 tbsp.)

Steps Used to Prepare:
1. Heat the Air Fryer to reach 350º Fahrenheit.
2. Slice the racks of lamb into quarters. Slice a deep pocket in each of the chops and stuff with thinly sliced cheese pieces.
3. Add a sage leaf on top and wrap with sliced prosciutto.
4. Spritz using one tablespoon of the oil. Set the timer for 15 minutes.
5. Transfer to a platter and serve.

Breaded Coconut Shrimp

Servings: 4

Ingredients:
- Shrimp (1 lb.)
- Panko breadcrumbs (1 cup)
- Shredded coconut (1 cup)
- Eggs (2)
- All-purpose flour (.33 cup)

Steps Used to Prepare:
1. Set the temperature of the Air Fryer at 360º Fahrenheit.
2. Peel and devein the shrimp.
3. Whisk the seasonings with the flour as desired. In another dish, whisk the eggs, and in the third container, combine the breadcrumbs and coconut.
4. Dip the cleaned shrimp into the flour, egg wash, and finish it off with the coconut mixture.
5. Lightly spray the basket of the fryer and set the timer for 10-15 minutes.
6. Air-fry until it's a golden brown before serving.

Breaded Cod Sticks

Servings: 5

Ingredients:
- Large eggs (2)
- Milk (3 tbsp.)
- Breadcrumbs (2 cups)
- Almond flour (1 cup)
- Cod (1 lb.)

Steps Used to Prepare:
1. Heat the Air Fryer at 350º Fahrenheit.
2. Prepare three bowls; one with the milk and eggs, one with the breadcrumbs (salt and pepper if desired), and another with almond flour.
3. Dip the sticks in the flour, egg mixture, and breadcrumbs.
4. Place in the basket and set the timer for 12 minutes. Toss the basket halfway through the cooking process.
5. Serve with your favorite sauce.

Cajun Salmon

Servings: 1-2

Ingredients:
- Salmon fillet (1 - 7 oz.) 0.75-inches thick
- Cajun seasoning
- Juice (¼ of a lemon)
- Optional: Sprinkle of sugar

Steps Used to Prepare:
1. Set the Air Fryer at 356º Fahrenheit to preheat for five minutes.
2. Rinse and dry the salmon with a paper towel. Cover the fish with the Cajun coating mix.
3. Place the fillet in the air fryer for seven minutes with the skin side up.
4. Serve with a sprinkle of lemon and dusting of sugar if desired.

Cajun Shrimp

Servings: 4-6

Ingredients:
- Tiger shrimp (16-20/1.25 lb.)
- Olive oil (1 tbsp.)
- Old Bay seasoning (.5 tsp.)
- Smoked paprika (.25 tsp.)
- Cayenne pepper (.25 tsp.)

Steps Used to Prepare:
1. Set the Air Fryer at 390º Fahrenheit.
2. Cover the shrimp using the oil and spices.
3. Toss them into the Air Fryer basket and set the timer for five minutes.
4. Serve with your favorite side dish.

Cod Fish Nuggets

Servings: 4

Ingredients:
- Cod fillet (1 lb.)
- Eggs (3)
- Olive oil (4 tbsp.)
- Almond flour (1 cup)
- Gluten-free breadcrumbs (1 cup)

Steps Used to Prepare:
1. Warm the Air Fryer at 390º Fahrenheit.
2. Slice the cod into nuggets.
3. Prepare three bowls. Whisk the eggs in one. Combine the salt, oil, and breadcrumbs in another. Sift the almond flour into the third one.
4. Cover each of the nuggets with the flour, dip in the eggs, and the breadcrumbs.
5. Arrange the nuggets in the basket and set the timer for 20 minutes.
6. Serve the fish with your favorite dips or sides.

Creamy Salmon

Servings: 2

Ingredients:
- Chopped dill (1 tbsp.)
- Olive oil (1 tbsp.)
- Sour cream (3 tbsp.)
- Plain yogurt (1.76 oz.)
- Salmon (6 pieces)/.75 lb.)

Steps Used to Prepare:
1. Heat the Air Fryer and wait for it to reach 285º Fahrenheit.
2. Shake the salt over the salmon and add them to the fryer basket with the olive oil to air-fry for 10 minutes.
3. Whisk the yogurt, salt, and dill.
4. Serve the salmon with the sauce with your favorite sides.

Crumbled Fish

Servings: 2

Ingredients:
- Breadcrumbs (.5 cup)
- Vegetable oil (4 tbsp.)
- Egg (1)
- Fish fillets (4)
- Lemon (1)

Steps Used to Prepare:
1. Heat the Air Fryer to reach 356º Fahrenheit.
2. Whisk the oil and breadcrumbs until crumbly.
3. Dip the fish into the egg, then the crumb mixture.
4. Arrange the fish in the cooker and air-fry for 12 minutes.
5. Garnish using the lemon.

Easy Crab Sticks

Servings: 2-3

Ingredients:
- Crab sticks (1 package)
- Cooking oil spray (as needed)

Steps Used to Prepare:
1. Take each of the sticks out of the package and unroll it until the stick is flat. Tear the sheets into thirds.
2. Arrange them on a baking tray and lightly spritz using cooking spray. Set the timer for 10 minutes.
3. *Note*: If you shred the crab meat, you can cut the time in half, but they will also easily fall through the holes in the basket.

Fried Catfish

Servings: 3

Ingredients:
- Olive oil (1 tbsp.)
- Seasoned fish fry (.25 cup)
- Catfish fillets (4)

Steps Used to Prepare:
1. Heat the Air Fryer to reach 400º Fahrenheit before fry time.
2. Rinse the catfish and pat dry using a paper towel.
3. Dump the seasoning into a sizeable zipper-type bag. Add the fish and shake to cover each fillet. Spray with a spritz of cooking oil spray and add to the basket.
4. Set the timer for 10 minutes. Flip, and reset the timer for ten additional minutes. Turn the fish once more and cook for 2-3 minutes.
5. Once it reaches the desired crispiness, transfer to a plate, and serve.

Avocado and Bacon Fries

Servings: 2

Ingredients:
- Egg (1)
- Almond flour (1 cup)
- Bacon – cooked – small bits (4 strips)
- Avocados (2 large)
- *For Frying*: Olive oil

Steps Used to Prepare:
1. Set the Air Fryer at 355º Fahrenheit.
2. Whisk the eggs in one container. Add the flour with the bacon in another.
3. Slice the avocado using lengthwise cuts. Dip into the eggs, then the flour mixture.
4. Drizzle oil in the fryer tray and set the timer for 10 minutes per side before serving.

Bacon-Wrapped Hot Dogs

Servings: 8

Ingredients:
- Bacon strips (8)
- Hot dogs (8)

Steps Used to Prepare:
1. Wrap each hot dog with the desired amount of bacon.
2. Place four hot dogs at a time in the Air Fryer basket. Space them so air can circulate.
3. Set the fryer to 360º Fahrenheit. Set the timer for 15 minutes.
4. Check to see if they are as you like them. If not, air-fry for another one or two minutes.

Cheesy Hot Dogs

Servings: 2

Ingredients:
- Hot dogs (2)
- Hot dog buns (2)
- Grated cheese (2 tbsp.)

Steps Used to Prepare:
1. Heat the Air Fryer for four (4) minutes at 390º Fahrenheit.
2. Arrange the hot dogs in the Air Fryer and cook for five minutes.
3. Place the hot dog on the bun and top it off with cheese.
4. Place in the fryer for about two minutes to melt the cheese and serve.

Jalapeno Poppers

Servings: 4-5

Ingredients:
- Jalapeno peppers (10)
- Fresh parsley (.25 cup)
- Cream cheese (8 oz.)
- Breadcrumbs (.75 cup)

Steps Used to Prepare:
1. Warm the Air Fryer at 370º Fahrenheit.
2. Slice the peppers into halves and deseed.
3. Combine the cream cheese and half of the crumbs. Sprinkle in the parsley.
4. Stuff each of the peppers and press the rest of the crumbs on the top for coating.
5. Set the timer and air-fry for 6-8 minutes or until they are nicely browned.

Mozzarella Cheese Sticks

Servings: 5

Ingredients:
- Mozzarella string cheese (10 pieces)
- Italian breadcrumbs (1 cup)
- Egg (1)
- Flour (.5 cup)
- Marinara sauce (1 cup)

Steps Used to Prepare:
1. Warm the Air Fryer at 400º Fahrenheit.
2. Toss the breadcrumbs, salt, and pepper.
3. Prepare three dishes. Dip each piece of cheese in flour, egg, and lastly the breadcrumbs.
4. Chill the sticks for one hour to help them hold the stick shape during frying.
5. Lightly spritz the sticks with coconut oil using a baking brush.
6. Arrange the prepared sticks in the Air Fryer. Set the timer for 8 minutes. At that point, turn them over using tongs and air-fry for another 8 minutes.
7. Wait for five minutes and transfer them from the pan to serve.

Pigs in a Blanket

Servings: 4

Ingredients:
- Crescent rolls (8 oz. can)
- Cocktail franks (12 oz. pkg.)

Steps Used to Prepare:
1. Warm the Air Fryer at 330º Fahrenheit.
2. Rinse and dry the franks using paper towels.
3. Slice the dough into rectangular strips (1.5 inches x 1-inch).
4. Roll the dough around the franks, but leave the ends open.
5. Place them in the freezer for approximately five minutes. T
6. Transfer them to the fryer for 6-8 minutes.
7. Raise the temperature setting to 390º Fahrenheit. Continue cooking for approximately three more minutes.

Potato Skin Wedges

Servings: 6

Ingredients:
- Russet potatoes (6 medium)
- Paprika (1.5 tsp.)
- Canola oil (2 tbsp.)
- Black pepper and salt (.5 tsp. each)

Steps Used to Prepare:
1. Wash the potatoes and boil in salted water for forty minutes.
2. Place them in the fridge to chill for about half an hour. Slice them into quarters when they have cooled.
3. Whisk the salt, paprika, pepper, and oil in a mixing dish.
4. Toss the potatoes in the mixture and arrange them in the cooking basket with the skin side down.
5. Air-fry them 14-16 minutes.

Sweet Potato Fat-Free Fries

Servings: 1-2

Ingredients:
- Sweet potatoes (1-2)
- Red potatoes (1-2)
- Optional: Parsley

Steps Used to Prepare:
1. Set the temperature to 356º Fahrenheit.
2. Peel and slice the potatoes. Toss into a container of water until ready for frying.
3. Towel-dry the wedges and spray using a baking oil spray.
4. Arrange a single layer of fries in the basket and set the timer for ten minutes.
5. Give the fries a shake, return to the Air Fryer for another eight to ten minutes.
6. Serve them the way you like them.

Air-Fried Plantains

Servings: 4

Ingredients:
- Avocado or sunflower oil (2 tsp.)
- Ripened/almost brown – plantains (2)
- *Optional*: Salt (.125 tsp.)

Steps Used to Prepare:
1. Warm up the Air Fryer to 400º Fahrenheit.
2. Slice the plantains at an angle for a .5-inch thickness.
3. Mix the oil, salt, and plantains in a container – making sure you coat the surface thoroughly.
4. Set the timer for eight to ten minutes; shake after five minutes. If they are not done to your liking, add a minute or two more.

Air-Fried Smores

Servings: 4

Ingredients:
- Whole graham crackers (4)
- Marshmallows (2)
- Chocolate - such as Hershey's (4 pieces)

Steps Used to Prepare:
1. Break the graham crackers in half to make eight squares. Cut the marshmallows in half crosswise with a pair of scissors.
2. Place the marshmallows cut side down on four graham squares. Place marshmallow side up in the basket of the Air Fryer and cook on 390° Fahrenheit for four to five minutes, or until golden.
3. Remove them from the fryer and place a piece Break all graham crackers in half to create eight squares. Cut marshmallows in half crosswise with a pair of scissors.
4. Place the marshmallows, cut side down, on four graham squares of chocolate and graham square on top of each toasted marshmallow and serve.

Apple Chips

Servings: 2

Ingredients:
- Cinnamon (.5 tsp.)
- Apple (1)
- Sugar (1 tbsp.)
- Pinch kosher salt (1 pinch)

Steps Used to Prepare:
1. Warm the Air Fryer in advance to reach 390º Fahrenheit.
2. Slice the apples lengthwise and arrange them in a dish with the cinnamon, sugar, and salt. Toss.
3. Cook them until they are crispy or around seven to eight minutes. Turn halfway through the cycle.
4. Transfer to a platter and serve.

Banana Smores

Servings: 4

Ingredients:
- Bananas (4)
- Mini-peanut butter chips (3 tbsp.)
- Graham cracker cereal (3 tbsp.)
- Mini-chocolate chips - semi-sweet (3 tbsp.)

Steps Used to Prepare:
1. Heat the Air Fryer in advance at 400º Fahrenheit.
2. Slice the un-peeled bananas lengthwise along the inside of the curve. *Don't slice through the bottom of the peel.* Open slightly - forming a pocket.
3. Fill each pocket with chocolate chips, peanut butter chips, and marshmallows. Poke the cereal into the filling.
4. Arrange the stuffed bananas in the fryer basket, keeping them upright with the filling facing up.
5. Air-fry until the peel has blackened, and the chocolate and marshmallows have toasted (6 minutes).
6. Chill for 1-2 minutes. Spoon out the filling to serve.

Cherry Pie

Servings: 8

Ingredients:
- Cherry pie filling (21 oz. can)
- Milk (1 tbsp.)
- Refrigerated pie crusts (2)
- Egg yolk (1)

Steps Used to Prepare:
1. Warm the fryer at 310º Fahrenheit.
2. Poke holes into the crust after placing it in a pie plate. Allow the excess to hang over the edges. Place in the Air Fryer for five (5) minutes
3. Transfer the basket with the pie plate onto the countertop. Fill it with the cherries. Remove the excess crust.
4. Cut the remaining crust into ¾-inch strips - weaving a lattice across the pie.
5. Make an egg wash using the milk and egg. Brush the pie. Air-fry for 15 minutes. Serve with a scoop of ice cream.

Easy Bacon

Servings: 8

Ingredients:
- Bacon (12 oz.)

Steps Used to Prepare:
1. Set the Air Fryer temperature at 350º Fahrenheit for ten minutes.
2. Arrange the bacon in a single layer in the Air Fryer.
3. Set the timer for 10 minutes.
4. Check for the desired crispiness and air-fry for an additional one to two minutes.
5. Between the batches, drain the grease. Serve as desired.

Fluffy Peanut Butter Marshmallow Turnovers

Servings: 4

Ingredients:
- Filo pastry (4 defrosted sheets)
- Chunky peanut butter (4 tbsp.)
- Melted butter (2 oz.)
- Marshmallow fluff (4 tsp.)
- Sea salt (1 pinch)

Steps Used to Prepare:
1. Set the temperature of the Air Fryer at 360º Fahrenheit.
2. Use the melted butter to brush one sheet of the filo. Put the second sheet on top and brush it also with butter. Continue the process until you have completed all four sheets.
3. Cut the layers into four—12-inch x 3-inch strips.
4. Place one teaspoon of the marshmallow fluff on the underside and one tablespoon of the peanut butter.
5. Fold the tip over the filo strip to form a triangle, making sure the filling is completely wrapped.
6. Seal the ends with a small amount of butter. Place the completed turnovers into the Air Fryer for three to five minutes.
7. When done, they will be fluffy and golden brown.
8. Add a touch of sea salt for the sweet/salty combo.
9. *Notes*: The Filo/Phyllo pastry is a little different than regular pastry. It is tissue-thin and has very little fat content. It is considered okay by some bakers and is interchange the filo with regular puff pastry for turnovers.

Funnel Cake Bites

Servings: 8

Ingredients:
- Greek yogurt (1 cup)
- Self-rising flour (1 cup - divided)
- For Dusting: Powdered sugar
- Optional: Vanilla bean paste (1 tbsp.)

Steps Used to Prepare:
1. Heat the Air Fryer at 375° Fahrenheit.
2. Combine the yogurt, ¾ of the flour, and vanilla if using.
3. Roll out the dough using the remainder of the flour.
4. Slice it into 32 squares and place in the Air Fryer (8 at a time).
5. Set the timer for 4 minutes. Flip then over and continue to air-fry for another 3 to 4 minutes until ready.
6. Lightly dust with the sugar as desired and serve.

Healthy Pop-Tarts

Servings: 6

Ingredients:
- Strawberries (.33 cup or 8 oz. - quartered)
- Granulated sugar (.25 cup)
- Refrigerated pie crusts (14.1 oz. pkg. Use 1)
- Powdered sugar (.t cup/2 oz.)
- Lemon juice (1.5 tsp./1 lemon)

Steps Used to Prepare:
1. Stir the strawberries and granulated sugar in a medium-sized microwavable bowl. Let the mixture stand for 15 minutes, stirring occasionally. Microwave on high until shiny and reduced, about 10 minutes, stirring halfway through cooking. Cool completely, about 30 minutes.
2. Roll the pie crust into a 12-inch circle on a lightly floured surface. Cut the dough into 12 rectangles (2.5 x 3-inch), rerolling scraps, as needed.
3. Spoon about two teaspoons strawberry mixture into center of six of the dough rectangles, leaving a .5-inch border. Brush the edges of filled dough rectangles with water, top with remaining dough rectangles, pressing edges with a fork to seal. Coat tarts well with a cooking oil spray.
4. Place three tarts in a single layer in the Air Fryer basket, and cook at 350° Fahrenheit or until it's golden brown (10 min.). Repeat with remaining tarts.
5. Place on a wire rack to cool completely, about 30 minutes.
6. Whisk the powdered sugar and lemon juice in a small bowl until smooth. Spoon the glaze over cooled tarts.
7. If you want, add a few candy sprinkles.

Molten Lava Cakes

Servings: 4

Ingredients:
- Eggs (2)
- Unsalted butter (3.5 oz.)
- Baker's Sugar - not powdered (3.5 tbsp.)
- Self-rising flour (1.5 tbsp.)
- Dark chocolate - chopped pieces (3.5 oz.)
- Also Needed: 4 Standard-sized oven-safe ramekins and microwave-safe bowl

Steps Used to Prepare:
1. Warm the Air Fryer to 375° Fahrenheit.
2. Grease and flour the ramekins.
3. Melt the butter and chocolate in the microwave for 3 minutes using "7" (3 min.) stirring thoroughly.
4. Whisk the sugar and eggs until the mixture is pale and frothy.
5. Mix the chocolate mixture with the egg mixture. Sift and mix in the flour.
6. Fill the ramekins about ¾ of the way to full with the cake. Set the timer for 10 minutes.
7. Remove them from the fryer and cool in ramekins for two minutes.
8. Flip the ramekins upside down onto a plate, tapping the bottom to loosen edges. The center should appear dark/gooey.
9. Serve warm with a raspberry drizzle.

Plain Cheesecake

Servings: 15

Ingredients:
- Unsalted butter (2 tbsp.)
- Honey graham cracker crumbs (1 cup)
- Cream cheese (1 lb.)
- Large eggs (2)
- Vanilla extract (.5 tsp.)

Steps Used to Prepare:
1. Set the Air Fryer to reach 350º Fahrenheit.
2. Cut a hole in the center of a piece of parchment paper and place it into the baking dish.
3. Combine the graham cracker crust and the butter. Press the mixture into the baking pan. Air-fry for four minutes
4. Blend the sugar and cream cheese with a mixer, adding one egg at a time until the mixture is creamy. Pour in the vanilla and stir well.
5. Pour the cheese mixture into the top of the crust and place it back into the Air Fryer for 15 minutes lowering the heat to 310º Fahrenheit.
6. Place in the fridge for about three hours before serving.

Yogurt Pineapple Sticks

Servings: 4

Ingredients:
- Pineapple (half of 1)
- Desiccated coconut (.25 cup)
- *The Dip:*
- Fresh mint (1 small sprig)
- Vanilla yogurt (1 cup)

Steps Used to Prepare:
1. Warm the Air Fryer to reach 392º Fahrenheit.
2. Slice the pineapple into stick segments. Dip the chunks of pineapple into the coconut. Arrange the sticks of pineapple into the cooker basket and air-fry for ten minutes.
3. Dice the mint into fine pieces and mix in with the yogurt.
4. Empty the dip into a serving dish. Arrange the baked sticks around the dip to serve.

CPSIA information can be obtained
at www.ICGtesting.com
Printed in the USA
LVHW060323261121
704499LV00011B/436